Moses

MARGARET HODGES

Moses

Illustrated by

BARRY MOSER

Harcourt, Inc.
ORLANDO ♦ AUSTIN ♦ NEW YORK ♦ SAN DIEGO ♦ TORONTO ♦ LONDON

The author gratefully acknowledges Rabbi James Gibson of Temple Sinai,
Pittsburgh, Pennsylvania, for his assistance in the creation of this book.
The illustrator wishes to thank Robert Willig, Dan Harper, Emily Crowe, and
Shalom Goldman for their invaluable help in the preparations for the images.

Requests for permission to make copies of any part of the work should be submitted
online at www.harcourt.com/contact or mailed to the following address:
Permissions Department, Harcourt, Inc.,
6277 Sea Harbor Drive,
Orlando, Florida 32887-6777.

www.HarcourtBooks.com

Library of Congress Cataloging-in-Publication Data
Hodges, Margaret.
Moses/Margaret Hodges; illustrated by Barry Moser. — 1st ed.
p. cm.
Summary: Retells the story of Moses, from his birth and trip in a boat of bulrushes to his bringing
of the Ten Commandments down from Mount Sinai.
1. Moses (Biblical leader)—Juvenile literature.   2. Bible. O.T.—Biography—Juvenile literature.
3. Bible stories, English—O.T. Pentateuch. [1. Moses (Biblical leader). 2. Bible stories—O.T.]
I. Moser, Barry, ill. II. Title.
BS580.M6H63 2006
222'.109505—dc21   97-005099
ISBN-13: 978-0-15-200946-5
ISBN-10: 0-15-200946-9
First edition
A C E G H F D B

PRINTED IN SINGAPORE

For all the walkers headed toward the promised land
—M. H.

And for my friends Karl and Kathy Donfried
—B. M.

IT BEGINS WITH A BABY IN A LITTLE BOAT

THIS IS THE STORY OF A LONG JOURNEY, AND IT BEGINS
WITH A BABY IN A LITTLE BOAT.

L ONG, LONG AGO, in the days
when the people of Israel were slaves in Egypt, a mighty pharaoh ruled
the land. He had the power of life and death over his slaves.

The people of Israel—the Hebrews—had always been shepherds, and
some still tended their sheep and goats in Goshen, the eastern part of
Egypt. But many were bound to rich masters in the fields and vineyards
of Egypt's great Nile River valley. Some labored in the desert making
bricks of clay and straw to build Pharaoh's cities, and some slaved in his
stone quarries. Under the harsh rule of Pharaoh and the Egyptians, the
Hebrews were often worked to death.

But all the while, they had hope.

They remembered that they had once lived in a country of their
own, Canaan. It was a land of green pastures and clear water, a land

so abundant it was said to flow with milk and honey. Their God had promised that someday they could go back to Canaan and live in freedom if only they would be faithful to him.

FOUR HUNDRED YEARS passed, and still freedom did not come. The Hebrews in Egypt grew in number. Pharaoh began to fear them. What if they joined with one of Egypt's enemies and overthrew his kingdom? He gave an order that all new Hebrew boy babies should be drowned in the Nile River as soon as they were born.

IN A TENT near the great river, a baby was born to a Hebrew couple. They had two other children, Miriam and Aaron. The baby was a boy, and although his mother hoped to hide him at home, she was terrified that Pharaoh's soldiers would hear him cry and take him away. Praying that a miracle might save her baby, she gathered bulrushes from the riverbank and wove them into a little boat, which she sealed tight with mud and tar, lined with soft grass, and fitted with a loosely woven lid.

The next morning she gave her sleeping baby one last kiss and laid him in the boat, setting it among the river reeds and rushes. Miriam hid nearby to keep watch.

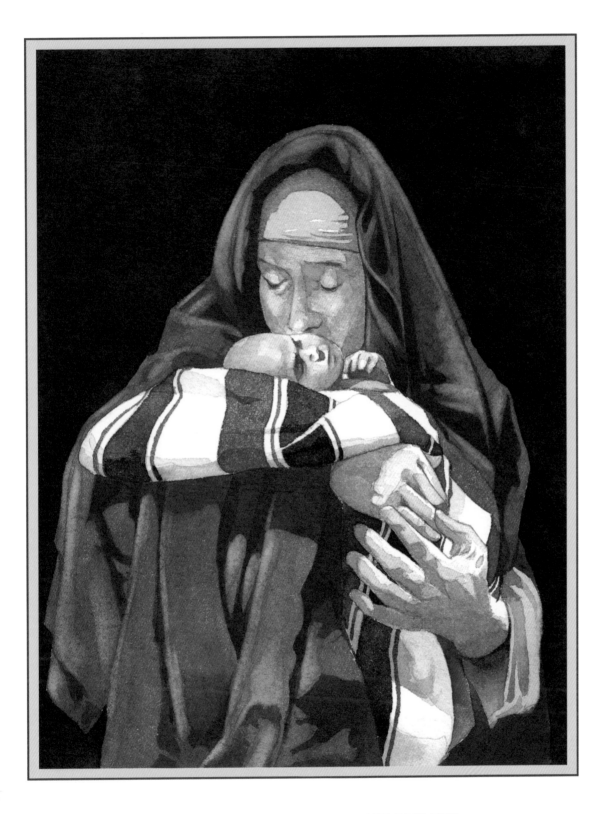

SHE GAVE HER SLEEPING BABY ONE LAST KISS

In the cool of the day, Pharaoh's daughter came down to the river to bathe. The princess saw the little boat among the bulrushes and told one of her maids to bring it to her. When the lid was raised, the baby awoke. He began to cry, and the heart of the princess was touched.

"This must be a Hebrew child whose mother has tried to save his life," she said. "He is a beautiful boy. Somehow I will protect him from my father's cruel order."

Miriam ran from her hiding place and knelt at the feet of Pharaoh's daughter. Trembling, she said, "Princess, I know a woman who would nurse the baby. May I bring her here?"

And when the mother came, her face full of love and fear, Pharaoh's daughter knew that the child must be hers. "Take care of this baby as if he were your own," the princess said. "When he is old enough to live safely in the palace rooms, he will be my adopted son."

So IT WAS DONE. The child was raised in the palace as a young prince, one of the royal family. And when anyone asked Pharaoh's daughter, "Who is he?" she answered only, "He came from the waters. His name is Moses, and he is my son."

THE CHILD WAS RAISED IN THE PALACE AS A YOUNG PRINCE

MOSES SAW AN EGYPTIAN SLAVE DRIVER BEATING A HEBREW

But Moses knew that his true family were Hebrew slaves living in a tent by the river.

As Moses grew up, he learned to worship the Lord God of the Hebrew people and bitterly felt their misery in Egypt. Day by day his silent anger against Pharaoh grew, but when he tried to speak of this to other people, he could not. He stuttered. His words came easily only when he spoke to God.

Then one day Moses saw an Egyptian slave driver beating a Hebrew who lay helpless on the ground. In a rage Moses killed the Egyptian and buried the body in a shallow grave. No one else had seen it happen, but the grateful slave told friends how Moses had saved his life.

Word reached Pharaoh that Moses was a despised Hebrew and now an outlaw. "Find him," Pharaoh said. "He must be put to death."

Moses fled from Egypt to a distant country. There he lived quietly among Hebrew shepherds. He married and became the father of two sons.

But Moses was not meant to live out his life as a peaceful shepherd.

MOSES SAW A MYSTERIOUS BURNING BUSH

Travelers brought news that the old pharaoh had died and that the new pharaoh was even more cruel. The suffering of the Hebrews in Egypt was desperate, and they had no leader who dared to speak for them.

ONE DAY, AS HE WAS tending his flocks in a pasture where grass was thin, Moses saw a mysterious burning bush. Amid a blaze of flames and fierce heat, the bush did not die, and from within the flames Moses heard the voice of an angel speaking words from God: "Moses, I see the sorrows of my people in Egypt, and I send you to set them free. Lead them out of Egypt to Canaan, the land I have promised them."

Moses answered, "Lord, how can I do this? Pharaoh will not listen to me. Not even my own people will listen. I do not speak well. I am a man of action, not of words."

But God said, "You will lead them. Take with you only your shepherd's rod. Use it to show signs and wonders so that people will know I am with you. As for words, your brother, Aaron, has grown to be a great speaker. He will find ways for you to speak to Pharaoh."

So it came about that the brothers met again. Moses told Aaron of the great task God had given them. Then they set off on the road back to Egypt, each carrying a shepherd's rod but no other weapon.

Aaron found the right words to inspire the people of Israel, and they learned by heart the secret plan: Moses would lead them out of slavery.

The day came when the brothers and the elders of Israel entered Pharaoh's great hall. They bowed low before him, saying, "The Lord God of Israel has sent us to you with this message: 'Let my people go out of Egypt and into the wilderness to offer sacrifice to me.'"

Pharaoh was scornful. "Who is this lord? If he is a god, show me a sign. I do not know him. Give me proof."

"Show thy power, Lord God!" Aaron cried. He threw his rod on the ground and it became a live serpent. All of Pharaoh's court drew back in fear. As they watched, Aaron picked up the serpent and it became a rod again.

Pharaoh's face did not change. "It is a trick," he said. "My wizards can do such things. Here is my answer: I will not let your people go. And I will no longer supply straw for your brick makers to mix with the clay. Let them find straw for themselves, and they must make as many bricks as ever."

IT BECAME A LIVE SERPENT

But the Hebrew slaves could not find enough straw. They made fewer bricks, no matter how hard they worked. When they begged Pharaoh for mercy, he said only, "Obey my will on pain of death!"

THEN HORROR CAME ON Egypt. The water of the Nile turned to blood, so that no one could drink it. Worse plagues followed. Frogs swarmed into the houses of the Egyptians, even into their beds. Lice were everywhere. Flies covered the land. The animals of the Egyptians fell sick with a deadly disease. Boils broke out on the bodies of both men and beasts. A storm of hail fell, beating down the crops in the fields. Locusts ate every leaf from every plant. Then thick darkness reigned day and night. Sun, moon, and stars disappeared.

As each plague came, God protected the Hebrews. Moses told Pharaoh that the plagues were a warning from the Lord God of Israel, and each time, Pharaoh said, "If the god of Israel will take away this plague, I will let the people go."

But each time, Pharaoh broke his promise.

God spoke again to Moses. "I shall bring one more plague. I shall pass through Egypt, and the firstborn of every Egyptian family will die. Each Hebrew family shall kill a lamb for their supper, and their doorways

HORROR CAME ON EGYPT

THEIR DOORWAYS SHALL BE MARKED WITH THE BLOOD

shall be marked with the blood. I shall pass over the homes marked with the blood of the lamb, and the Hebrew firstborn will be saved. Tell my people to eat unleavened bread and bitter herbs with the lamb and to keep the feast of the Passover each year forever in remembrance of this great night when I myself will lead my people out of Egypt."

God's words spread to every Hebrew family, and they obeyed, while in every Egyptian family there was weeping and wailing. Pharaoh was terrified. He called Moses to him and cried, "Go! Be gone, and take all your people with you."

QUICKLY AND QUIETLY, the people of Israel ate their last supper in slavery and began the long journey to the east, to the promised land of Canaan. And every day a pillar of cloud went before them to guide them. Every night a pillar of fire lighted their road.

From his royal palace Pharaoh looked out in wrathful despair. He had lost his firstborn child on the night of Passover. And when he saw his empty brickyards and stone quarries, he knew he could never replace the Hebrew men who had labored there so long and so hard. He would break his promise to the people of Israel once again.

Pharaoh gave orders. Six hundred of his fastest horses were harnessed, each chariot bearing a driver and a bowman. Pharaoh himself stepped into his own splendid chariot, ready to follow with the rest of the army. At his signal, the first chariots set off, racing at full speed, to where the Hebrews would cross the Red Sea. Before they could build boats or rafts to escape, the Egyptian armies would overtake them.

THE HEBREWS WERE camped on the shore of the Red Sea when they heard the distant thunder of hooves and chariot wheels. Pharaoh's chariots! The people were filled with fear and cried out to Moses, "Why did you not let us stay in Egypt? It was better to be alive there, even as slaves, than to die here!"

Moses answered, "Fear not. The Lord will fight for you, and you will never see the Egyptians again."

Night fell. The angel of God that had led the people as a cloud by day and a fire by night moved behind them and hid them. The Egyptian army lost sight of the Hebrews and stopped to wait for dawn's light.

In the darkness, as Moses stood by the shore, God spoke again: "Lift up your rod and stretch it toward the sea."

"Lord God, help us!" Moses cried, and a strong east wind began to

THE ANGEL OF GOD HID THEM

MOSES BEGAN TO WALK ALONG THAT PATH

blow. With every hour it blew stronger. It rose in force until nothing could be heard but its roar. It swept back the waves of the Red Sea, leaving a dry path between walls of water from shore to shore.

*I*N THE MORNING Moses began to walk along that path, and the people followed. Pharaoh was furious to see that his slaves would soon be safe on the farther shore.

"Forward!" he shouted. Trumpets blared and six hundred charioteers lashed their horses. Into the pathway they galloped. But God threw the Egyptians into confusion. The frightened horses reared and plunged, throwing the riders from the chariots.

When the Hebrews had reached safety, Moses again stretched out his rod over the sea. Then, above the shouts of charioteers and bowmen, another sound was heard—the roar of waves. The great walls of water trembled, and fell. Pharaoh's chariots, horses, and riders disappeared forever into the depths of the sea.

MOSES'S SISTER, MIRIAM, gathered together the women of Israel. They danced and sang in thanksgiving:

I will sing unto the Lord, for he has triumphed gloriously;
The horse and his rider he has thrown into the sea. . . .
The chariots of Pharaoh he has cast into the sea.

So ISRAEL CAME out of Egypt. Hunger and hardship still lay between them and the promised land, but with God's help, Moses found food in the wilderness. It was Moses who learned from God the laws by which his people should live in order to become worthy of the promised land. It was Moses who climbed alone to the top of Mount Sinai and brought back God's Ten Commandments, cut into tablets of stone. Before the end of his life, Moses chose new leaders, young and wise and strong, to guide the people onward. When he closed his eyes for the last time, he was still looking toward the promised land, flowing with milk and honey, and it was in sight.

Moses was at peace. His long journey was over, and God had been with him all the way.

GOD HAD BEEN WITH HIM ALL THE WAY

THE TEN COMMANDMENTS

א

YOU SHALL have no other gods before me.

ב

YOU SHALL not make any graven images;

you shall not bow down to them, nor serve them.

ג

YOU SHALL not take the name of the Lord your God in vain.

ד

REMEMBER the sabbath day, to keep it holy.

ה

HONOR your father and your mother.

ו

YOU SHALL not kill.

ז

YOU SHALL not commit adultery.

ח

YOU SHALL not steal.

ט

YOU SHALL not bear false witness against your neighbor.

י

YOU SHALL not covet anything that is your neighbor's.

Moses

The illustrations in this book were executed in transparent watercolor

on a mold-made watercolor paper from Le Moulin d'Arches mills in France.

The display lettering was created by Judythe Sieck.

The text type is Matthew Carter's Galliard,

inspired by the classic sixteenth-century French typefaces of Robert Granjon.

The Hebrew on page twenty-nine is Le Bé, designed by Matthew Carter

and based on Hebrew letters cut by Guillaume Le Bé,

a contemporary of Granjon.

This use of modern Hebrew is in contrast to the ancient Hebrew

portrayed in the illustrations on pages twenty-seven and twenty-eight.

Color separations by Bright Arts Ltd., Hong Kong

Printed and bound by Tien Wah Press, Singapore

This book was printed on 104gsm Cougar Opaque Natural paper.

Production supervision by Jane Van Gelder

Designed by Barry Moser and Judythe Sieck